CONTENTS

THE TRAGEDY OF POMPEII

About 2,000 years ago, Pompeii was a bustling, prosperous city. It enjoyed warm sunshine, blue sea and green fertile land. A few kilometres from Pompeii, Mount Vesuvius quietly peered over the city and its people. It was a peaceful and happy region.

Then disaster struck. In twenty-four hours of terror, Pompeii was completely destroyed. To discover the tragedy of Pompeii, let's visit the city in August AD 79, just before the catastrophe occurred.

This is Mount Vesuvius today. It is a volcano, 1,281 metres high.

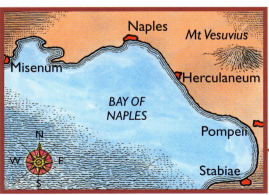

Pompeii nestled along the Bay of Naples on the west coast of modern-day Italy. Misenum, Naples, Herculaneum and Stabiae also overlooked the bay.

B   e

INCLUDES
ACTIVITY SHEET

Series Literacy Consultant
Dr Ros Fisher

Pearson Education Limited
Edinburgh Gate
Harlow
Essex CM20 2JE
England

www.longman.co.uk

ISBN 978 0 582 84125 3

Colour reproduction by Colourscan, Singapore
Printed and bound in China (GCC/04)

The Publisher's policy is to use paper manufactured from sustainable forests.

Fourth impression 2009

The following people from **DK** have
contributed to the development of this product:
Art Director Rachael Foster

Martin Wilson **Managing Art Editor**	**Managing Editor** Marie Greenwood
Kath Northam **Design**	**Editorial** Hannah Wilson
Helen McFarland **Picture Research**	**Production** Gordana Simakovic
Richard Czapnik, Andy Smith **Cover Design**	**DTP** David McDonald

Consultant Philip Wilkinson

Dorling Kindersley would like to thank: Rose Horridge in the DK Picture Library; Ed Merrit for cartography; and Johnny Pau for additional cover design work.

J937.
7

LIFE IN POMPEII

In AD 79 Pompeii was, for many people, a perfect place to live. Farmers became wealthy by growing olives or grapes, and merchants made money selling cloth or wool. But while the rich people enjoyed luxurious lives, others were poor and their daily lives were a struggle.

aureus (gold)

sestertius (brass)

denarius (silver)

Roman coins

A ROMAN TOWN

Pompeii was part of the Roman Empire. General Sulla and his Roman army had conquered the city in 89 BC. From that time, the people of Pompeii were Roman citizens.

Soon Pompeii became an important trading centre, shipping its produce to other parts of the Roman Empire. Rome defended Pompeii from attack. Under the protection of Rome, the people of the city felt safe.

Roman soldiers protected Pompeii from attack.

Roman Empire in AD 117

Britain

France

Italy

Rome

Turkey

Spain

Greece

MEDITERRANEAN SEA

Egypt

Rome and its armies conquered many territories around the Mediterranean Sea.

CITY LIFE

About 20,000 people lived within Pompeii's network of streets. Pompeii was surrounded by massive walls with eight heavily guarded gates and eleven watchtowers.

Public life in Pompeii, like any Roman city, was focused around the forum. This was the town square – a large open space where people carried out their daily business. Merchants traded their goods while politicians made speeches from platforms.

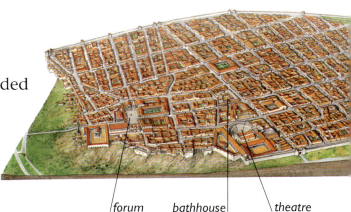

forum   bathhouse   theatre

The walled city of Pompeii

Pompeii's forum

temple of Apollo, the Roman god of the Sun, music and poetry

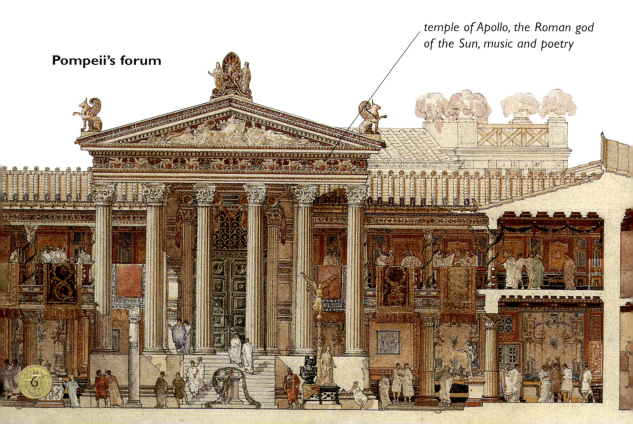

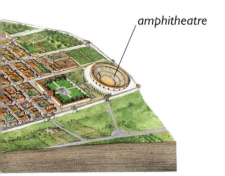
amphitheatre

Magnificent buildings, such as the law courts and the huge temples with their grand colonnades and spectacular statues, bordered the forum. Shops and market stalls packed the forum.

The forum was not just a place of business. It provided an impressive stage for musicians and poets. Often people gathered in the forum just to catch up on the latest gossip.

Poets recited their work to anyone who would stop to listen.

temple of Jupiter, the ruler of all the Roman gods

THE LIVES OF THE RICH

Away from the busy crowds of the forum, the wealthy people of Pompeii enjoyed the peace and quiet of their grand, spacious houses. These houses were designed for luxurious living. They had huge airy halls and beautiful gardens with shady walkways.

Houses were furnished and decorated with goods from Greece, Spain, North Africa and Syria that were regularly unloaded at the nearby port of Stabiae.

Wealthy ladies owned beautiful objects like this silver mirror.

A Roman house in Pompeii

statue in the entrance hall, or atrium

walkway

gardens often contained water fountains or ponds

A mosaic is a picture or pattern made from small pieces of stone or tile. This mosaic warned visitors to beware of the dog.

Rooms were decorated with beautiful mosaics or wall paintings. Many of the paintings illustrated stories about the gods and goddesses that the people worshipped. A dining-room wall might have displayed a picture of a bowl of plump, juicy apricots and grapes. In the hall, lively scenes from the forum might have decorated a wall.

One of the most important pastimes that took place in the home was entertaining guests. Romans loved to throw long, rowdy dinner parties. Fish, lobster and eel from the Mediterranean Sea was often on the menu. Meals were made up of twelve small courses and took four hours to eat.

celery

herbs

fish

Typical ingredients used in Pompeii

Romans lay on couches and ate with their fingers when dining.

THE LIVES OF THE POOR

Many poor people lived in Pompeii. They lived in blocks of flats called *insulae*, which is the Latin word for "islands". Insulae were often several storeys high and had shops on the ground floor. Families crowded into tiny flats with no running water or cooking facilities. Poor people bought food from street stalls, markets and local bars.

Children often played jacks on the streets below the blocks of flats.

Slaves often helped their masters buy *amphorae* (jars) filled with olive oil or wine at the markets.

Among the poor of Pompeii was a large slave population. As the Roman armies conquered new lands, they captured millions of people and made them slaves. Some masters treated their slaves very badly, but others taught them reading and mathematics so the slaves could be more useful.

WARNING SIGNS

During the few days before disaster struck, Vesuvius sent warnings to the people of Pompeii that something terrible was about to happen. But the people ignored the signs and carried on as usual. This mistake cost many of them their lives.

This stone carving shows the damage caused to Pompeii in an earthquake in AD 62.

RUMBLINGS

Mid-August in AD 79 was unbearably hot in Pompeii. One day, when there was no wind at all, hanging lamps began to sway.

Then pots and pans began to clatter about on shelves, and the earth trembled. The citizens were used to rumblings in the land surrounding Vesuvius, so they weren't worried.

There had been a serious earthquake seventeen years earlier in AD 62, but the city had been repaired and most people had forgotten about it. Anyway, the people had no reason to think that these tremors had anything to do with their volcano, Vesuvius.

Vulcan is the Roman god of fire and metal working. Vulcan gave his name to *vulcanus*, which is the Latin word for "volcano".

Not everyone was so calm. High on the slopes of Vesuvius, the farmers were worried. Far from the hustle and bustle of the city centre, they could sense that unusual activities were taking place deep inside the volcano. Their animals could sense this, too. When their sheep became afraid, the farmers knew something was very wrong.

People were too busy with their daily life to listen to the warnings of the farmers.

What is a Volcano?

A volcano is a mountain formed over an opening in the Earth's crust. Underneath the volcano, magma (hot liquid rock), gases and steam collect. This creates an immense pressure that can force the magma to the surface, producing a volcanic eruption. The movement of the magma can cause tremors in the ground above.

feeder pipe   magma

The farmers ran down from the countryside to warn the citizens, but their warnings were ignored.

Flocks of seagulls flew away from the city, and pet birds fluttered nervously in their cages. Water stopped flowing from the public fountains.

Even if the people noticed these signs, they may not have understood what they meant. All the danger signs were ignored.

BUSINESS AS USUAL

The next day, shopkeepers, merchants and
customers continued buying, selling, talking
and laughing. Perhaps they noticed the ground
trembling now and then, but it didn't interfere
with their daily lives, so why worry?

Modestus the baker and his slaves continued
baking bread in a huge oven and selling it from
a shop next door. Like most people in Pompeii,
he was too busy to pay attention to rumblings
from Vesuvius.

Men and women relaxed in the bars that
lined the streets. They drank the local wine
and chatted happily to each other.

Streetside bars
sold wine, nuts,
olives, bread,
cheese and onions.

handle

flask
of oil

strigil

Romans didn't use
soap. They rubbed their
bodies with oil and then
scraped the oil and dirt
away with a thin, metal
tool called a *strigil*.

People also visited the public bathhouses. Public baths were busy, noisy places and an important part of Roman life. Romans liked to be clean and well-groomed. They looked after their health and took pride in their appearance.

People didn't visit the baths just to wash. They also went to meet friends, do business and relax.

There were three public bathhouses in Pompeii and each one had a variety of rooms. There were cold rooms, warm rooms, hot rooms and changing rooms. Men and women bathed separately, so many different rooms were needed.

**Public bathhouse
in Pompeii**

A worker who was too busy to go to the baths could visit the barber in the forum for a quick trim. This was a social event, as passersby often stopped to chat.

*shops along the
front of the baths*

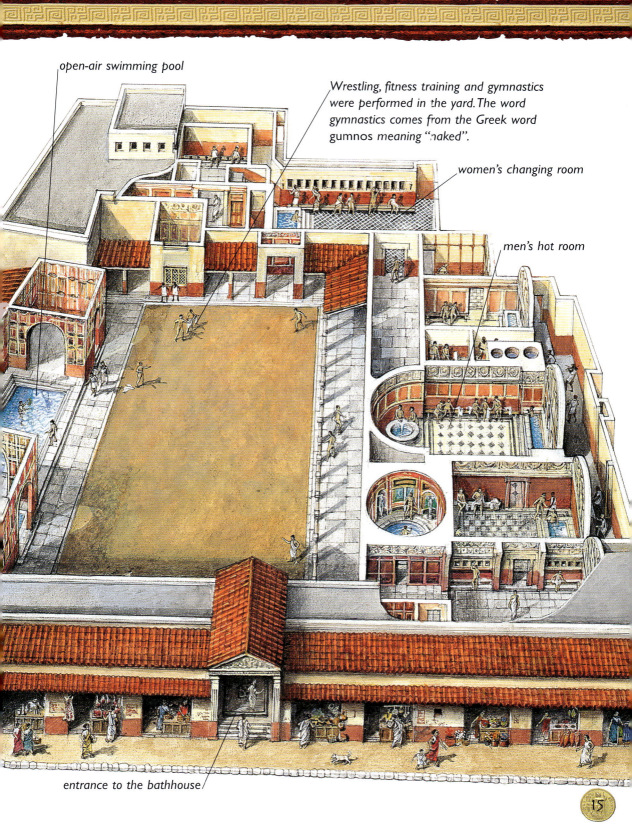

open-air swimming pool

Wrestling, fitness training and gymnastics were performed in the yard. The word gymnastics comes from the Greek word *gumnos* meaning "naked".

women's changing room

men's hot room

entrance to the bathhouse

On the day before the disaster, the citizens watched plays in the open-air theatre. It often staged pantomimes, in which the story was told with movement and dance, not words.

About 5,000 spectators squeezed onto the stone steps that rose in a huge horseshoe-shape around the stage. People brought cushions to make themselves more comfortable. Wealthy citizens carried tickets made from bone that allowed them to sit in the front rows.

The word *theatre* comes from the Greek word *theatron*, meaning "a place for watching".

Gladiators were usually slaves or criminals.

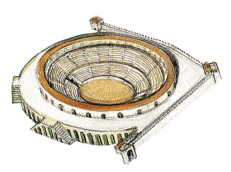

Gladiator battles took place in an amphitheatre. In Greek, *amphi* means "around". An amphitheatre has seats all around the arena.

The amphitheatre was even more popular than the theatre. Twenty thousand bloodthirsty spectators flocked there to watch gladiators fight in the arena. (The word *gladiator* comes from the Latin word *gladius*, which means "sword".)

ERUPTION

24 August AD 79 began like any other day. No one could have imagined the horror with which it would end.

That morning, Modestus the baker kept watch over his slaves as they baked their loaves of bread. Actors and gladiators performed in front of large crowds and, in the baths, people chatted to each other as they washed.

The people of Pompeii spent the morning completely unaware of the destruction that was about to be unleashed from Vesuvius.

Then suddenly, at about mid-day ...

BOOM!

A thunderous explosion shook Pompeii. It was more deafening than anything that had ever been heard before. People inside shops and houses rushed out in terror. Everyone in the streets stared up in horror at Mount Vesuvius.

The top of Vesuvius had disappeared. A churning column of black smoke rose into the sky. People stood, shocked, unable to believe their eyes. Then they realized that the huge black cloud was moving their way.

Greyish ash began to fall like dirty snowflakes. Chunks of pumice (light stones filled with air bubbles) spattered down.

Vesuvius Erupts

A volcanic cloud of dust, pumice and ash rose more than 20 kilometres into the air.

smoke rose vertically before being blown sideways by the wind

The explosion caused panic among all the citizens, rich or poor. The bakery workers fled, clutching the day's takings. Rich women were helped to escape by slaves.

PANIC!

People ran this way and that. Some frantically searched for loved ones, while others ran away as fast as they could.

Actors performing in the theatre had their words drowned out by the mighty explosion. Dressed in their costumes, they fled the stage as the audience scrambled for the exits.

In the bakery, Modestus' workers stopped what they were doing and ran for their lives. Gladiators had to decide whether to shelter inside their lodgings or race for safety. Those who stayed died.

SUFFOCATING SMOKE

During the next few hours, the growing black cloud gradually blotted out the Sun while the terror-stricken citizens of Pompeii fled.

When the first storm of ash and pumice began to fall, most citizens fled instantly. It's possible that up to 18,000 people escaped by moving quickly. However, many people delayed, fumbling and groping in the dark for treasured possessions. Soon the air became so thick with dust and gas that those who lingered suffocated and died in their homes.

Places where ash fell

Naples

Mt Vesuvius

most ashfall

Herculaneum

Pompeii

BAY OF NAPLES

N W E S

least ashfall

The wind blew the cloud away from Herculaneum but directly towards Pompeii.

The ash and pumice that fell from Vesuvius in the first few hours after the eruption was light and did not crush the citizens. Instead people were suffocated by the poisonous fumes as they tried to flee.

PLINY THE ELDER INVESTIGATES

At about 2:30 pm, a woman, who was at home in Misenum on the other side of the Bay of Naples, saw a strange cloud in the distance. She ran to tell her brother, Pliny the Elder. Pliny could see that the cloud was rising from a mountain, but he was too far away to know that it was Vesuvius. He needed to get closer.

Pliny the Elder was a naval commander and he ordered a boat to sail him across the bay towards the mysterious giant cloud.

Pliny the Elder's nephew, Pliny the Younger, wrote two letters to the famous historian Tacitus. In these letters, Pliny the Younger described his uncle's journey in great detail.

Pliny the Younger's description of the cloud:

"It rose into the sky like an immense tree with spreading branches."

As Pliny was getting ready to set sail, a messenger brought him a letter. It was from his friend Rectina, who lived at the foot of Vesuvius. Her life was in danger and the only way to escape was by sea. She desperately needed Pliny's help.

Pliny's journey of investigation had become a rescue mission. He ordered more boats so that he could try to rescue as many people as possible.

PLINY SETS SAIL

As Pliny sailed with his ships across the bay towards the black cloud, he quickly realized that there had been a volcanic eruption from Vesuvius. Hot ash, pumice and burning stones rained down.

As the boats neared the shore volcanic debris blocked their path. Pliny decided to continue farther around the bay to Stabiae where some friends lived.

Pliny spent the night in Stabiae, which had not yet been hit by the terrors in Pompeii.

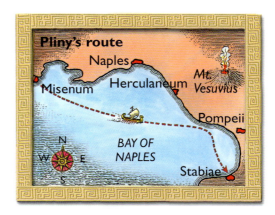

Pliny's route

Naples

Misenum

Herculaneum

Mt. Vesuvius

Pompeii

BAY OF NAPLES

N W E S

Stabiae

Debris from Vesuvius

pumice (light volcanic rock)

The sea was churned up by the debris that Vesuvius was hurling into it.

volcanic ash

volcanic dust

lapilli (small chunks of lava)

22

BURIED – DEAD OR ALIVE

As Pliny's boats were trying to reach Pompeii, conditions in the city were getting worse. The downpour from Vesuvius was increasing and becoming heavier. Rocks and burning stones hailed onto the city streets among the clouds of dust and ash.

As night fell, a thick layer of debris coated Pompeii, causing buildings to collapse. The people who had not suffocated in the poisonous air were buried alive.

Friction from dust particles produced lightning, which cracked across the dark sky. Vesuvius continued to belch out fiery lava throughout the night. But there was worse to come ...

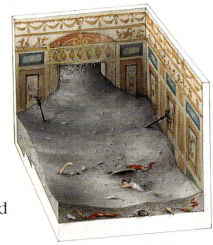

Thick layers of ash preserved bodies for almost 2,000 years.

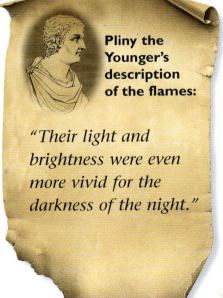

Pliny the Younger's description of the flames:

"Their light and brightness were even more vivid for the darkness of the night."

A NEW TERROR

About midnight, the towering column of smoke that had been spurting out of Vesuvius collapsed. It formed a deadly avalanche of gas, dust, ash, lava and pumice. This fiery flow swept down the slopes of Vesuvius at an incredible speed.

The nearby town of Herculaneum had escaped the worst of the ashfall, but it was the first to be destroyed by this new terror. The avalanche swept through the town at about 100 kilometres per hour, destroying everything in its path. In less than four minutes, the whole of Herculaneum was wiped out. Luckily, almost everyone had already escaped. But thirty men and women were still sheltering in Herculaneum's harbour. They were burned alive by the ferocious heat of the flow. The heat was so great that the sea began to boil.

Pompeii was next ...

Mount Vesuvius last erupted in 1944.

Pyroclastic Flow

When the column of smoke collapsed, it formed an avalanche of hot gases and fiery volcanic material. This is called a pyroclastic flow.

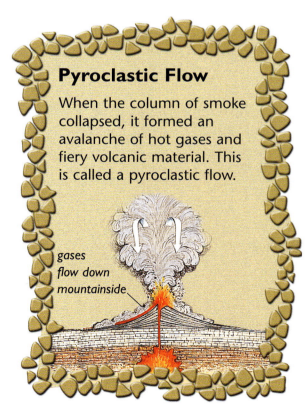

gases flow down mountainside

A DREADFUL DAWN

Despite the horrors that were taking place during the night, Pliny slept well in Stabiae. His snores were heard from outside his room. When Pliny woke on the morning of 25th August and looked outside, he saw that the courtyard was buried in ash and stone. Debris from Vesuvius had reached as far as Stabiae. If Pliny had slept any longer, he would have been trapped – possibly buried alive.

Pliny knew that he and his friends were in trouble. It was dangerous to go outside into the storm of ash and pumice, but it was equally dangerous to stay indoors because tremors were shaking the house.

Calmly, Pliny decided that they should leave the house. If they reached the harbour, they could escape by sea.

Wild seas prevented anyone from escaping in boats from Stabiae.

25

THE FINAL MOMENTS

Pliny and his friends held lanterns to light their way to the shore through the dark smoke.

When they reached the beach, Pliny could barely breathe in the hot, dust-laden air. He lay down and pleaded for water. His chest heaved with the strain of breathing the poisonous air. Soon afterwards, Pliny the Elder collapsed and died.

Friends and slaves of Pliny tied cushions to their heads to protect themselves from the falling debris. They tried to help Pliny.

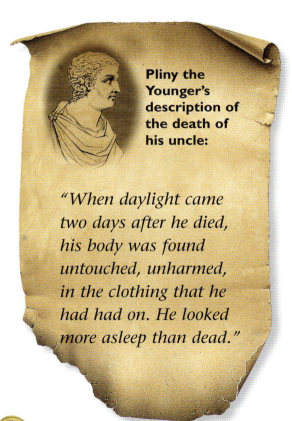

Pliny the Younger's description of the death of his uncle:

"When daylight came two days after he died, his body was found untouched, unharmed, in the clothing that he had had on. He looked more asleep than dead."

For Pliny, the horror of the eruption had come to an end. But what of the city of Pompeii?

At 7:30 am, a huge and violent pyroclastic flow had swept over the ash-covered city. In less than two minutes, the burning avalanche of gas and stone killed any people who still survived. The flow completely buried the city, which lay cushioned in its thick layer of ash and pumice.

Pompeii had disappeared.

POMPEII UNCOVERED

For hundreds of years, Pompeii was forgotten. The pyroclastic flow had covered the ash-covered city with a thick blanket of debris. This debris had hardened over the years, preserving the city like a time capsule. Pompeii was buried under a layer about 6 to 7 metres thick. It was invisible to those who walked over it.

This painting of 1799 shows the excavations at Pompeii. The horseshoe-shaped theatre is on the right.

Then in 1709, a man digging a well in the countryside near Vesuvius discovered some pieces of marble. The excavation of Pompeii began.

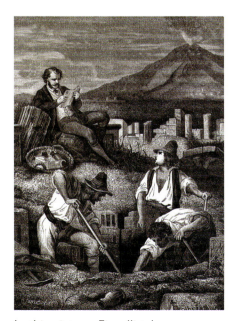

In this picture, Fiorelli takes notes and instructs workers about how to excavate.

THE WORK OF FIORELLI

Fortune hunters came to the site of Pompeii, lured by the promise of buried treasure. For the next hundred years, people dug frantically at the site, scavenging Roman treasures and damaging the ancient buildings.

Fortunately, in 1864, an Italian archaeologist called Giuseppe Fiorelli took charge of the excavations. He organized a system to excavate Pompeii and to preserve its ruins. The location of every item found was carefully recorded.

Giuseppe Fiorelli is best remembered for discovering the people of Pompeii. His team of archaeologists carefully dug out Pompeii, working downwards, layer by layer. Slowly a few roofs were revealed, then walls and floors. At floor level, they found cavities. Fiorelli realized that these cavities were the spaces left by decomposed bodies. Only the skeletons remained, lying in their hollow tombs.

Plaster casts were made for animals, too. This is Rufus, a guard dog.

Fiorelli filled each cavity with plaster and then chipped away the surrounding rock. This produced plaster casts of the people who had died on that dreadful day. Their clothes, hair – even the expression on their faces – could be seen.

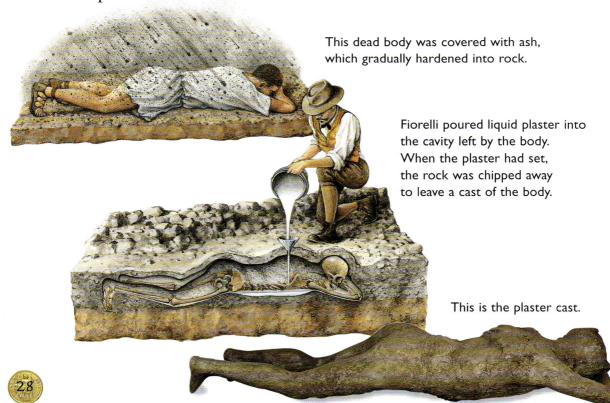

This dead body was covered with ash, which gradually hardened into rock.

Fiorelli poured liquid plaster into the cavity left by the body. When the plaster had set, the rock was chipped away to leave a cast of the body.

This is the plaster cast.

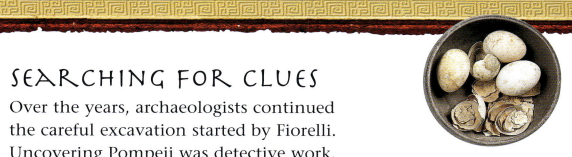

SEARCHING FOR CLUES

Over the years, archaeologists continued the careful excavation started by Fiorelli. Uncovering Pompeii was detective work, and archaeologists continually discovered clues about daily life in a city stopped in time.

These eggs were found in a temple.

Paintings and mosaics that had decorated the walls and floors of homes, temples and bars were found. Artwork shows how people lived, who they worshipped, how they thought and how they liked to pass the time.

Archaeologists found food that had been preserved for almost 2,000 years. In Modestus' bakery, they found eighty-one loaves of bread that had been baked on the morning of the eruption.

This loaf of bread was turned into charcoal.

Workers were carefully supervised during excavations in the late 19th century.

BURIED TREASURE

Excavating Pompeii produced some very exciting Roman remains. Public buildings and the homes of wealthy citizens of Pompeii were filled with great treasures. Bronze statues, marble carvings and jewellery made with gold, silver and emeralds have all been found. These treasures are even more valuable today than they were in Roman times. Each one tells a story about the past.

This gold coiled snake was worn as an armband.

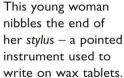

This young woman nibbles the end of her *stylus* – a pointed instrument used to write on wax tablets.

This is a statue of Eumachia, who was one of the most important women in Pompeii.

Graffiti was found on walls all over Pompeii. People wrote about their favourite gladiators, and children often wrote comments about their teachers.

POMPEII TODAY

Today archaeologists continue their work in Pompeii. They want to discover everything that the city has to reveal. Pompeii still holds secrets from almost 2,000 years ago. Archaeologists hope to learn more about Pompeii and the Roman world. They also hope to find out more about the men, women and children who lived in the city and who died on that fateful day in AD 79.

Vesuvius looks quiet today, but deep inside the volcano, it still smoulders. Scientists keep an eye on volcanic activity. Hopefully they will predict an eruption if one should occur ever again.

Herculaneum has been only partly excavated because the modern town of Resina is built on top of it.

Today visitors to Herculaneum walk along the streets of a city frozen in time.

INDEX